Squawk

squawk

For Patrick and Ben
(the noisiest and best!)

ACKNOWLEDGMENTS

The publisher gratefully acknowledges permission to use the following material:

On the Ning Nang Nong by Spike Milligan, from *Silly Verse for Kids,* published by Puffin Books. **Ears Hear** © 1964 by Lucia and James L. Hymes, Jr., from *Oodles of Noodles,* reprinted by permission of Addison-Wesley Publishing Company, Inc. **Laughing Time** © 1990 by William Jay Smith, reprinted from *Laughing Time: Collected Nonsense,* by permission of Farrar, Straus & Giroux, Inc. **Commissariat Camels** reprinted by permission of A. P. Watt Ltd. on behalf of The National Trust for Places of Historic Interest or Natural Beauty. **Quack, Quack!** © 1979 by Dr. Seuss Enterprises, L P, from *Oh, Say Can You Say?* reprinted by permission of Random House, Inc. **"Quack!" Said the Billy Goat** © by Charles Causley, from *Figgie Hobbin,* published by Pan Macmillan. **Kitchen Sink-Song, Early Walkman,** and **City Music** © 1997 by Tony Mitton, reprinted by permission of Murray Pollinger Literary Agent. **Our Washing Machine** © 1963, 1991 by Patricia Hubbell, reprinted by permission of Marian Reiner for the author. **The Small Ghostie** © by Barbara Ireson, from *Rhyme Time,* published by Hamlyn. **Steel Band Jump Up** © by Faustin Charles, reprinted by permission of M. C. Martinez Literary Agency. **Fishes' Evening Song** © 1967 by Dahlov Ipcar, reprinted by permission of McIntosh & Otis, Inc. **The Sound Collector** © by Roger McGough, from *Pillow Talk,* published by Viking, reprinted by permission of Peters, Fraser & Dunlop.

Library of Congress Cataloging-in-Publication Data

Poems go clang! : a collection of noisy verse / illustrated by Debi Gliori.
—1st U.S. ed.
Summary: A collection of short poems, such as "Quack, Said the Billy Goat," "Kitchen Sink-Song,"
"New Shoes," and "City Music," which feature all sorts of sounds.
ISBN 0-7636-0148-9
1. Sound—Juvenile poetry. 2. Noise—Juvenile poetry. 3. Sounds—Juvenile poetry.
4. Children's poetry, American. 5. Children's poetry, English.
[1. Sound—Poetry. 2. Poetry—Collections.]
I. Gliori, Debi, ill.
PS593.S67P64   1997
811.008'09282—dc20   96-30750

2 4 6 8 10 9 7 5 3 1

Printed in Italy

This book was typeset in Kozmik Plain One and Kozmik Plain Two. The pictures were done in watercolor and ink.

Candlewick Press
2067 Massachusetts Avenue
Cambridge, Massachusetts 02140

POEMS GO CLANG!

A Collection of Noisy Verse

Illustrated by Debi Gliori

CANDLEWICK PRESS

CAMBRIDGE, MASSACHUSETTS

On the Ning Nang Nong

On the Ning Nang Nong
Where the Cows go Bong!
And the Monkeys all say Boo!
There's a Nong Nang Ning
Where the trees go Ping!
And the tea pots Jibber Jabber Joo.
On the Nong Ning Nang
All the Mice go Clang!
And you just can't catch 'em when they do!

6

Ears Hear

Flies buzz,
Motors roar.
Kettles hiss,
People snore.
Dogs bark,
Birds cheep.
Autos honk: *Beep! Beep!*

Winds sigh,
Shoes squeak.
Trucks honk,
Floors creak.
Whistles toot,
Bells clang.
Doors slam: *Bang! Bang!*

Kids shout,
Clocks ding.
Babies cry,
Phones ring.
Balls bounce,
Spoons drop.
People scream: *Stop! Stop!*

Lucia and James L. Hymes, Jr.

BUZZzzzzzz

toot!

CLANG!

woof!

creak!

SQUEA

Laughing Time

It was laughing time, and the tall Giraffe
Lifted his head, and began to laugh:
Ha! Ha! Ha! Ha!

And the Chimpanzee on the ginkgo tree
Swung merrily down with a Tee Hee Hee:
Hee! Hee! Hee! Hee!

"It's certainly not against the law!"
Croaked Justice Crow with a loud guffaw:
Haw! Haw! Haw! Haw!

The dancing Bear who could never say "No"
Waltzed up and down on the tip of his toe:
Ho! Ho! Ho! Ho!

Ha! Ha! Ha! Ha!

Tee Hee Hee Hee! Hee! Hee!

Haw! Haw! Haw! Haw!

The Donkey daintily took his paw,
And around they went:
Hee-haw! Hee-haw! Hee-haw! Hee-haw!

The Moon had to smile as it started to climb;
All over the world it was laughing time!
Ho! Ho! Ho! Ho! Hee-haw! Hee-haw!
Hee! Hee! Hee! Hee! Ha! Ha! Ha! Ha!

William Jay Smith

Quack, Quack!

We have two ducks. One blue. One black.
And when our blue duck goes "Quack-quack"
our black duck quickly quack-quacks back.
The quacks Blue quacks make her quite a quacker
but Black is a quicker quacker-backer.

Dr. Seuss

Commissariat Camels

We haven't a camelty tune of our own
To help us trollop along.
But every neck is a hairy trombone,
Rtt-ta-ta-ta! is a hairy trombone.
And this is our marching song:
Can't! Don't! Shan't! Won't!
Pass it along the line!

Rudyard Kipling

13

"Quack!" Said the Billy Goat

"Quack!" said the billy goat,
    "Oink!" said the hen.
"Miaow!" said the little chick
    Running in the pen.

"Hobble-gobble!" said the dog,
    "Cluck!" said the sow.
"Tu-whit-tu-whoo!" the donkey said,
    "Baa!" said the cow.

"Hee-haw!" the turkey cried,
　　The duck began to moo.
All at once the sheep went,
　　"Cock-a-doodle-doo!"
"Bleat! Bleat!" said the owl
　　When he began to speak.
"Bow-wow!" said the cock
　　Swimming in the creek.

"Cheep-cheep!" said the cat
　　As she began to fly.
"Farmer's been and laid an egg—
　　That's the reason why."

Charles Causley

15

Kitchen Sink-Song

Tap goes drip-drip
plip-plip-plink.
Tap goes trickle at the
kitchen sink.
Fridge goes gurgle.
Pan goes slop.
Bin goes flip-flap.
Toast goes POP!

Tony Mitton

DRIP
DRIP

FLIP~
FLAP

GURGLE

SLOP

Our Washing Machine

Our washing machine went whisity whirr
Whisity whisity whisity whirr
One day at noon it went whisity click
Whisity whisity whisity click
Click grr click grr click grr click
Call the repairman
Fix it . . . Quick!

Patricia Hubbell

POP

CLICK CLICK

WHISITY WHISITY WHISITY

The Small Ghostie

When it's late and it's dark
And everyone sleeps . . . shhh shhh shhh,
Into our kitchen
A small ghostie creeps . . . shhh shhh shhh.

We hear knocking and raps
And then rattles and taps,

Then he clatters and clangs
And he batters and bangs,
And he whistles and yowls
And he screeches and howls . . .

So we pull up our covers over our heads
And we block up our ears and
WE STAY IN OUR BEDS

Barbara Ireson

18

Auntie's Skirts

Whenever Auntie moves around
Her dresses make a curious sound;
They trail behind her up the floor,
And trundle after through the door.

Robert Louis Stevenson

New Shoes

My shoes are new and squeaky shoes,
They're very shiny, creaky shoes,
I wish I had my leaky shoes
That Mommy threw away.

I liked my old brown leaky shoes
Much better than these creaky shoes,
These shiny, creaky, squeaky shoes
I've got to wear today.

Anonymous

squeak

creak

21

Early in the Morning

Come down to the station early in the morning,
See all the railway trains standing in a row.
See all the drivers starting up the engines,
Clickety click and clackety clack,
Off they go!

Come down to the garage early in the morning,
See all the buses standing in a row.
See all the drivers starting up the engines,
Rumble, rumble, rumble, rumble,
Off they go!

Come down to the seaside early in the morning,
See all the motor-boats floating in a row.
See all the drivers starting up the engines,
Splishing, splishing, sploshing, sploshing,
Off they go!

Come down to the airport early in the morning,
See all the airplanes standing in a row.
See all the pilots starting up the engines,
Whirring, whirring, whirring, whirring,
Off they go!

Anonymous

Steel Band Jump Up

I put my ear to the ground,
And I hear the steel-band sound:
Ping pong! Ping pong!
Music deep, rhythm sweet,
I'm dancing tracking the beat;
Like a seashell's ringing song,
Ping pong! Ping pong!
Moving along, moving along,
High and low, up and down,
Ping pong! Ping pong!
Pan beating singing, round and round,
Ping pong! Ping pong!

Faustin Charles

City Music

Snap your fingers.
Tap your feet.
Step out a rhythm
down the street.

Rap on a litter bin.
Stamp on the ground.
City music
is all around.

Beep says motor-car.
Ding says bike.
City music
is what we like.

Tony Mitton

Early Walkman
(5 million years ago)

Fasten seashell
onto each ear.

Listen. Amazing!
What me hear?

Sound of water,
wind, and rain
washing about
inside my brain.

Stand on two legs.
Walk along.
Listening to
that seashell song.

Tony Mitton

Fishes' Evening Song

Flip flop,
Flip flap,
Slip slap,
Lip lap;
Water sounds,
Soothing sounds.

We fan our fins
As we lie
Resting here
Eye to eye.
Water falls
Drop by drop,

Plip plop,
Drip drop.
Plink plunk,
Splash splish;
Fish fins fan,
Fish tails swish,

Swush, swash, swish.
This we wish . . .
Water cold,
Water clear,
Water smooth,
Just to soothe
Sleepy fish.

Dahlov Ipcar

26

swish

fan

swush

swash

swish

The Sound Collector

A stranger called this morning
Dressed all in black and gray
Put every sound into a bag
And carried them away

The whistling of the kettle
The turning of the lock
The purring of the kitten
The ticking of the clock

The popping of the toaster
The crunching of the flakes
When you spread the marmalade
The scraping noise it makes

The hissing of the frying-pan
The ticking of the grill
The bubbling of the bathtub
When it starts to fill

The drumming of the raindrops
On the window-pane
When you do the washing-up
The gurgle of the drain

The crying of the baby
The squeaking of the chair
The swishing of the curtain
The creaking of the stair

A stranger called this morning
He didn't leave his name
Left us only silence
Life will never be the same.

Roger McGough